On April 6, 2010, my husban
devastating news that he had a ~~brain tumor. The following is an~~
account of his brain tumor journey, made up of posts that he and I
wrote to share updates with family and friends. To make it easier for
you to differentiate between our posts, my posts are italicized, and
John's are printed in normal text.

OUR STORY

*John had been having terrible headaches for a couple of weeks, and
went to the doctor, thinking he was having a migraine or sinus
infection. After a whirlwind day that included a CT scan and MRI,
we learned that he has a brain tumor. He is scheduled for surgery to
remove it on Monday April 19th. We won't know until after the
surgery exactly what type of cells are involved, and what the
treatment will be.*

*It appears to be a high grade primary tumor. This is good, as it
means it doesn't seem to have metastasised from somewhere else. It
is located in the back of his brain, behind his right ear. There is
only one tumor - also good. It's located in a part of the brain that
doesn't have a lot of function, (insert joke here!) so it's unlikely to
affect things like speech, mobility etc. It also is localized in one part
of the brain, and doesn't appear to have spread into more than one
lobe, and isn't near the brain stem.*

*The doctor is confident that she can remove the tumor successfully,
and without causing any damage.*

So, keep us in your thoughts and we will keep you posted.

*P.S. Well, the tumor is out, and the post surgery MRI looked good.
It was a nasty tumor, nicknamed "Rat Bastard Tumor" by John.
Treatment includes 6 weeks of radiation and chemotherapy and a
clinical trial drug, followed by chemo for 5 days out of every 28 for
a year.*

Here is a big shout out to Dr. Souza and Dr. Stanley at Harbor Medical.

These folks are awesome! I want to give all of you knuckleheads some very important information. Dr. Stanley told me that the reason they were able to identify this tumor so quickly is because " I presented my case so well". When Dr. Souza started asking me questions about my symptoms I laid it all out for her. First I told her everything I could think of. I did not hold back. I tried to recall anything that was out of the ordinary to provide her with enough information to begin the reasoning process. I guarantee if I had gone in to my appointment and held things back she would have given me a prescription for a sinus infection and that would be it. But since I gave her all of the details, it created enough questions that she believed that there could be an underlying root cause that she wanted to investigate. My first reaction was a little sanguine but I went along with it and thank goodness that I did.

So the take away here is please, please, please listen to your body, be clear and keep asking questions until it makes sense and hopefully it will save/mitigate your life or someone that's close to you.

One final note, I fully expect some funny posts on my web site.

Written Apr 16, 2010 7:16pm

Two long days of testing at the hospital. Yesterday was the functional MRI for the brain mapping, and the surgical MRI to help guide the doctor during surgery. John wishes the MRI machines were louder and that they could all play Frank Sinatra music all of the time.

Today was pre-op testing and lots of information about before, during and after surgery. Yikes...info overload. We expect that he will be in the hospital for about 4 days. It's a 5 hour surgery. He'll be in the ICU after the surgery on Monday and can only have short visits from family. Hopefully if all goes well, he will be moved out of the ICU on Tues morning, and can have visitors then.

We got to see some of the functional MRI results, and they are really positive. First, there is a brain in there....no sign of the sawdust and carpenter ants that John's been talking about. The MRI showed that all of his speech and other major functions are located in other parts of the brain, not near the tumor, so this is great news.

So, that's it for now. Spending a low key weekend, carb loading for the marathon on Monday.

Written Apr 19, 2010 12:22pm

Hello all,

John is out of surgery and evidently bothering everyone. The doctor has already told him to quiet down. The surgery went very well. Initial report confirms the primary brain tumor diagnosis, but we won't know what type until hopefully later this week.

He may be in ICU longer than planned as they try to get his blood pressure under control, but he's doing great so far. He really needs to rest and be quiet and give his brain a chance to recover, which as you all know, is very difficult for him. They are restricting his visitors for now, to keep him calm.

I haven't seen him yet, but will report back later after I've had a chance to see for myself that he's not turned into Frankenstein or something.

Written Apr 19, 2010 7:14pm

Thank you to Dr. Golby! John is doing so well. They will monitor him in the ICU overnight, and hopefully he'll be well enough to go to a regular unit tomorrow. So far, his sense of humor and personality are intact, and he seems like himself, only more so since he's on the steroids still. It's like John to the nth power, which is a bit overwhelming at times :)!

Now he has to try to rest and heal, and we have to continue to keep him a little quiet.

Thank you all for the prayers, positive thoughts, cards and notes. All of it helps so much. I'm feeling so relieved that this part of the ordeal is behind us, and we can now focus on healing, and then the next treatments.

Written Apr 25, 2010 9:40am

Hi all,

This is from John AKA Sweater, Sweaterdude, Nick, Claw, Dumbass and etc.

First- the serious part- all of the posts on this site have made me so happy. Reaching out like you have has been really inspirational. There is something so powerful when you feel the force of great people praying, thinking, directing good vibrations and etc. in your direction. It's inspiring to say the least.

Second part- I hope you all were able to take advantage of the extra Kohl's 15% savings available all day long during the grand opening event.

The surgeon- Dr. Golby is amazing. She is brilliant, is raising two small children and manages to keep a wonderful balance between work and home. She is a rock star +++++ (plus she is really cute).

At the tender age of 42, she has established the Golby Lab, a surgical brain mapping laboratory at Harvard Medical School and Brigham and Women's Hospital.

My long term plan is to adopt her as a niece to go along with other great nieces and nephews, awesome friends, family, neighbors, coworkers and customers.

Diagnosis- I have a very important story tell here. I won't go into detail now. This cancer was discovered early and it was part divine intervention/luck/good graces/gods will and etc.

Reader's Digest version- I listened to my body. I went to my primary care doctor. I presented my symptoms as clearly as possible and I told her everything including some crazy hallucinations that I had experienced.

The only way I could relate my experience was to ask the doctor if she had ever tried mushrooms when she was in college (by the way I did try it once and it was the scariest and most horrible experience). Naturally I was prepared for a WTF response but I also thought it was important for her to know what was going on.

Originally I thought that I had a headache from seasonal allergies. She prescribed an antibiotic but she said that because I presented my situation so well that a CT scan should be taken. After I had the CT scan I was called immediately for an MRI. When I arrived for my MRI I knew it was going to be bad because they only had Frank Sinatra music available. That was the MOST painful part of the process; 30 minutes of bad Sinatra - oh the inhumanity!

THE BIG TAKE AWAY FROM ABOVE IS THAT WHEN YOU GO TO YOUR DOCTOR, DON'T HOLD BACK. TRY TO THINK ABOUT WHAT'S GOING ON AND PERHAPS WRITE THINGS DOWN AHEAD OF TIME SO YOU DON'T FORGET ANY DETAILS.

I have so many funny things to tell you about this whole episode and here is just one.

After the operation I was in the 9th floor ICU. The doctor needed a new MRI to understand how the surgery went (to compare a before and after look at the tumor). There was a team of two tranport people and my nurse that needed to move me down 9 congested floors with crowded elevators, milling people, and etc. I was fully conscious; feeling myself and ready to have some laughs. So I ask the transporters if we encounter traffic would it be okay to start fake groaning in pain so that people would get out of the way.

One of the transporters laughed and, that was all of the encouragement I needed. Needless to say, John, the over the top clown, came out. Everytime we came to an intersection with people I started groaning and moaning and declaring major pain. We got through every major intersection first, got the first available elevator and laughed our butts off all the way down the MRI area.

That is just one of the things that happened to me.

I have truly been touched by angels and it's so wonderful.

Written Apr 27, 2010 8:02am

Hey all,

I am back for some good old fashioned trash talk.

First off, I love this web site but I am so used to the "Word" spell check, auto correct and etc. that I am totally unprepared to write without help. So I apologize in advance for spelling, capitalization, syntax errors and etc but it is what it is.

First- useful revelations
I am on steroids, which really amplifies who you are (oh frigging god) so as you know I have just the slightest tendency to be goofy and act like about 13 years old at the best.

The beauty of steroids is they are doing something to help me but they also give me boundless, and I mean boundless, energy. Additionally I feel like I can solve any problem and can fix any situation. My beautiful, patient, wicked smart wife has reminded me at least 20 times not to try to fix everyone and everything. I cannot wait to get weaned off these drugs because I have not been shy about telling people how they should run their lives. Needless to say, this is very dangerous and potentially really destructive to the people closest to you and I don't want to be a PITA more than usual.

The lesson- when people are on steroids for whatever reason, please know that they are not themselves and try to give them a pass wherever possible.

Next lesson- anyone that takes steroids to get bigger muscles and etc is playing with fire to the nth degree.

Enough with the life lessons now for some funny stuff.

Anesthesia/operation/what I remember:

On the morning of the surgery we met with the surgeon, Dr. Golby and the sleep man whose name is Dr. Knapp (too frigging funny). I actually liked that the man had a name that matched his profession.

The sedation process started with a little IV to relax me. The surgeon started to tell me what was going to happen. I told her that I had 1000% confidence in her and don't bother telling me anything unless she needed my help.

They placed a mask over my face and my final thought before complete and total unconsciousness was to suck on that mask as deeply as possible because the last thing I wanted to do was be in any state of awareness.

The next thing I remember was people calling my name and waking me up. As I opened my eyes it appeared to me that I was was being born again. Two things that occurred to me was first, since I looked down and saw my legs first I was thinking that my rebirth was actually a breach birth so my next thought was that having a 266 pound breach birth baby has got to hurt a lot more than my knock on head.

Prior to my discharge a representative from Dr. Knapp's department came to speak with me concerning my sedation. She began to ask me questions. Naturally in my elevated steroid state I thought I knew what she needed to know before she asked the questions. I am such a turd sometimes. Rather than letting her ask the questions I said, "let me tell you the experience and my current condition". I knew they would stick a tube into my lungs and I would have a little irritation and would be expectorating fluid. To the common folks that means I would have some funky luggies. She asked me to describe my total sedation experience to wit I said, "have you ever been to a keg party?" Naturally she said "NO".

Here is what I told her. The total experience was like a 1972 UMASS keg party. I showed up, imbibed heavily and woke up wondering WTF happened and where am I? I had a total cramp in my left butt cheek; a bang on the back of my head. What was missing was the smell of stale beer and a hangover. After that description she said that I had supplied all the information needed and literally ran out of my room. I actually started laughing and turned on the TV to one of my favorite programs "Sponge Bob Square Pants": - as you all know I am quite the intellectual.

Stay tuned many more stories to follow.

Additionally if you think that anyone anywhere might derive any benefit at all please send this link along to them because I would like help anyone that is in need of support because this is all new ground.

Rock on.

Written Apr 29, 2010 8:42am

Hey,

I hope all you folks are well. I will give you folks a quick health update then time for some funny stuff.

First- I feel "pretty, witty and wise", a quote from My Fair Lady. I admit it, I like musicals and my favorite musical is Oklahoma.

A quote- "Be your self because everyone else is taken"- Noel Coward

Actually I feel really great. From a pain perspective on a 0-10 the pain is 0. From a Terri Nickerson perspective the pain level has to be in the 8-10 area. Being around me is exhausting. The drugs (steroids) give me boundless energy and the urge to talk, so god bless Terri for patience, support and kindness.

Now on the plus side, I will let Terri report on my behavior. I have been clearing the table, doing the dishes, taking out the compost and etc. I love to take on any task. The bad news is that because of my surgery, lifting anything over 5-10 pounds would create an excess pressure on my brain which could undo some very sophisticated surgery.

This 5-10 pound limit on doing things is very, very, very challenging!!!!!!

I take great pride in my physical strength. I have always worked hard at being physically strong and active. Anyone that has played basketball or other sports with me knows I enjoy being physical but I am not a "cheap shot" kind of guy.

AT THIS POINT, I WOULD LIKE SOME OF MY OLD OCEAN SPRAY BASKETBALL FIRENDS TO COMMENT AND DON'T BE SHY, ESPECIALLY COLLIGAN aka Combie, FALLON AND MIKE MCENEMA.

MY FAMILY BACKGROUND- I am quite convinced that the Nickersons were the last family to descend from the trees. We are not as a whole very smart, but we did see that there were benefits from being ground dwellers at some level. So hopefully when this storm has passed I will be able to resume my normal activities which include but are not limited to:

-Dragging my knuckles on the ground
-Picking up heavy things over my head because I can
-Lifting my boat trailer tongue up to move the boat and trailer to the truck rather than backing the truck up to the boat and trailer, like a normal person would.

One of my favorite recent physical experiences occurred in 2007 and 2008. Terri and I bought some land on the Vineyard and had about 10 cords of logs to cut and split. To me this was heaven on earth, what a challenge! I enlisted my nephew Steven and other Homo Sapiens that like physical effort. I cannot tell you how many people saw the pile of logs and said such things as " you can sell them whole", "you can cut them up and rent a log splitter" and etc.

I got a lot of great advice but to me there is nothing more exciting than taking on a tough challenge with friends and family.

I love my chain saw and a sharp chain, making smooth cuts through the wood and etc. My next absolute joy is to split wood. There is a tool which is heaven sent for a monkey like me. It's called the "Monster Maul". My brother Charlie turned me onto this weapon of mass destruction about 20-25 years ago. At the time it was mail order and cost $19.95. The Monster Maul heretofore called the MM is 100% steel from top to bottom. I am not sure what the total weight is but it's certainly at least 20 -25 pounds. The biggest issue with the MM is that when you swing that tool at maximum force applying all of your effort, there is no coming back. If this is a mistake someone is gonna get hurt and it will leave a mark.

I really enjoyed reducing approx 10 cords of logs to nicely cut and and split firewood which I sold for $200/cord, you pick up. I did not do this chore alone. I had help from a lot of my homies including but not limited to:

Steven Nickerson- my nephew; a wonderful person so full of heart and giving- this dude has muscles on top of his muscles!

Stevie D- one of the best; this man has a heart as big as the ocean. Fishing with Stevie and his brothers is a total hoot. The best part is breakfast at Percy's after where we gather to basically talk smack.

Steve Torrey- one of the best friends a guy could have. Steve has an English background so he has just a little trouble with getting close to guys. I take advantage of this every chance I get to give him a hug. I can feel his skin crawl and it justs makes me so happy to make him so uncomfortable.

Scott Azer, my brother in law- I tip my hat to Scott especially since Terri's family descended from the trees a lot sooner than the Nickersons. He came down and busted out some serious wood. I know this was not a day at Disneyland for him.

Terri Nickerson- Terri watched some serious work get done. I have to also add that during this show I had two broken ribs #8 and 9. My nephew got angry and threw me down on the rocks one night while fishing (not really but it sounds cool). So if the wood did get cut and split it was due to the hard work of some great peeps.

Terri asked repeatedly if the could swing the MM. Since this thing is so heavy and she is a peanut she could only make the tiniest and I mean tiniest little dent in the wood. She would try so hard and we would laugh so hard and she kept trying. One day as if the lord granted her a wish she swung the old MM with all of her force and chipped off a tiny piece of wood approx three inches wide and 12 inches long. I forget how many people were there but we all laughed so hard. To this day I still have that piece of wood to remind me of how tough my girl is. You should have seen her face. It was like she won the frigging Nobel peace prize. Priceless!

More to follow- please if you think anyone would find any benefit in reading this drivel pass it along.

By the way, the doctor told me that writing helps remap the brain. It's sort of like the Boston big dig- it cost a lot of money, there are still traffic jams but basically information can pass or cars can travel more efficiently in a very congested area.

Hey,

I hope you are all well and I hope that I am not too boring.

First the health update then some more stuff from the early years.

Today is the day that my niece Elizebeth, Terri and I go to see Dr. Golby. I actually cannot wait to see her and tell her how much I like my scar. I wear this as the red badge of courage. I am feeling very strong. It's amazing how quickly the brain can heal; even my little brain stuffed into this big melon.

I have been thinking a lot about cancer and more broadly serious personal illness. My conclusion is that while I have cancer my entire family is affected with outward rippling effects. My wife, daughters, brother, sister, in-laws, out-laws, friends and etc. are all linked. I am sure that many or all of you have other friends and loved ones that are affected with cancer, heart disease and etc. and to that end you have my deepest sympathy and support.

Today's topic is bullying- it's in the news a lot lately and I want to give you my testimony on bullying.

As a kid I was bullied, yes bullied, really bullied, to the point where I always had my eyes peeled so that I could run, hide, go inside a store and seek protection because there was a group of older kids that wanted to whip my ass.

How it all began-

I am the youngest of 4 children: Bobby, Chickie, Kathy and Johnny.

The year is approx 1965. To set the stage, my sister Kathy is two years older than me and a real pissah. She has never taken crap from anyone. I am in 5th grade (10 or 11 years old) and she is in 7th grade (12 or 13 years old). Back then boys did not seem to hit girls but it was okay to even the score with other members of the offending family.

My sister was not always the most diplomatic person and could easily point out other people's short comings.

The stage is set. There are 3 kids in 7th grade that need to settle a score with a 5th grader named John Nickerson. To be honest, I have never been cool and really never wanted to be cool.

I think my dad found out that I was being chased, harrassed and generally was miserable because of bullies chasing me around town. One day my dad sat down with me and asked if kids were bothering me and I said yes. My dad's response was brilliant! He said, " John, bullies are cowards. They only have strength in numbers. You will never find a bully picking a fight alone because they are afraid and gutless". My dad said, "all you have to do is find one of these bullies alone and challenge them to fight right there. Maybe you will get a beating but maybe you will win. In any event, that bully will never pick on you again because you chose to stick up for yourself and the outcome of the next fight is never certain." The next words out of his mouth were, "be brave; it's not easy".

As luck would have it, I was walking home from the Washington Street park when I heard the bully (initials M.L.) yell at me, "hey Crisco". These bullies called me "Crisco"; you know fat in the can ha, ha. ML had snuck up on me with his fancy stingray bike. As it turned out ML was alone and wanted to have some fun with me. I thought of my dad's advice. ML got off his fancy stingray bike. He thought I was going to run or something but I had had enough and I said "let's go".

Back in the day, when you fought there were rules. First, boxing only, no weapons, gouging and etc. When the opponent got knocked down he was allowed to either stand up and continue or the fight was over. After the fight was over you shook hands and it was over. Second, during any fight you could declare aloud "anything goes" and that meant you were going to do anything possible to defend yourself.

We faced off on the side walk. ML had a 3-5 inch reach advantage. I could punch but I could not land a blow. I knew enough to keep my chin in but I caught two really hard punches to my left jaw. This kid tagged me. At that point I was totally pissed off. I declared "anything goes"! Being the uncool kid that I was, I was wearing a pair of Forrest Gump shoes. The shoes I wore were really stiff and heavy. When ML was planning his next jab I wound up my leg as hard as I could and kicked him perfectly in the middle of his shin. I swear I used every bit of power I had. No big surprise; ML hit the ground writhing in pain.

I took off running for home thinking the other bullies would be after me. I laid low for a week waiting for the heat to die down. On the very first day that I decided to walk to the park all three bullies surrounded me with their fancy stingray bikes. ML got off his fancy stingray bike and came up to me and said "do you know how hard you kicked me?" I said, "do you know how hard you hit me in my jaw?" I would like to say that we all became great friends and etc. but we did not. We established a truce. I was never bullied by those guys again. I would also like to add that 2 of those bullies went on to overdose on "H".

I have no idea how to deal with the bullying stuff that goes on today but certain things are true. Bullies are cowards. They only have strength in numbers. When you stand up for yourself people may not like you but by god they respect you.

Sorry for the long post but this type of writing takes my mind off of other things.

Hi all,

It's John with an update. I am sorry its been so quiet but Terri, my niece Beth, (the geneticist) and Dr. Barry Cuiffo (very dear personal friend that is head of oncology at a major hospital) have been doing a lot of thinking about my situation and next steps.

It's a bad news/good news situation.

First the bad news. This is a tough tumor. I refuse to honor it with a name so it's now called "Rat Bastard Tumor" or RBT.

Now the good news. Dr. Golby was very happy with the surgery. Basically she said the tumor had clean margins and lots of jargon that was good. The surgery was scheduled for 5 hours and it only took 3 so it was as good as could ever be expected.

The standard treatment for this type of tumor is 6 weeks of radiation and chemo simultaneously.

Additionally because I am so pretty, have great hair, am a great physical specimen, young age, good health background etc, several clinical trials were made available.

Each trial has pros and cons with long term implications for qualifying for additional new trials, new drug therapy and etc. It's truly mind boggling. It's sort of like the TV show "Let's make a Deal" with far reaching implications.

Please know that I am very happy with where we are at.

I have signed the research consent form for a trial and now I must qualify through some testing. I have 3 appointments tomorrow at the Dana Farber for various tests (good times).

You now have all of the details we are comfortable sharing.

And now its time for funny tales from the crypt.

This is a true story from my 10th grade summer.

I had just turned 16 years old on June 26, 1969. What a time to be a teenager in any part of the world except 41 Elliott Street in Reading, MA where I lived. My dad retired from the Navy as Chief Bosuns Mate. As anyone that served on a ship will tell you, the Navy has lots officers and etc. but it's the Chiefs that get things done.

My dad worked for the town of Reading on the Highway department. He had to be at the town garage by 7:30 for work, and he kept his work shoes on the attic staircase, which was accessed through my little tiny room which I shared with my brother Charlie. My dad approached the day as he did when he was in the Navy. Every morning at 06:30 my father would burst into the room and yell "its time to get up" without regard for vacations and even weekends.

I had been trying to find a full time job, but when you are a 16 year old kid without a driver's license you are neither fish nor fowl. My dad had the solution to my job search quest. A drinking buddy from the Reading V.F.W. had a construction company and was in need of a strapping young man that would work for peanuts.

Mr. Mike Enwright was president, CEO, Chairman and etc. To get hired I had to go through a very a rigorous hiring process. Mike dropped my dad off at home from the VFW one Saturday afternoon. I was cutting the grass and he walked up to me and said "you start on Monday. Be at the corner of route 28 and Knollwood Road at 8:00 am sharp. Don't be late. We are going to be doing some excavation and hooking up some houses to the town sewer system". To be honest, I thought he was a little sketchy because he had a brown paper bag duct taped to the truck door that said "Mike Enwright Construction" written with a magic marker . But I was in no position to question the judgment of my Chief Bosuns Mate father, especially after a few beers.

Day 1

I could not wait until Monday morning. I was pumped. In fact, I was getting dressed as my father walked into my room and yelled "its time to get up". I said" I am up" and he said "don't get wise with me". Now that's my dad.

I arrived promptly at 7:45 for my first day of work, so excited to be part of the construction industry and making a difference for all of the people without sewerage on Knollwood Road. I felt truly alive and purposeful. As it turned out Mike Enwright had a big Sunday night at the VFW and did not show up until 10 am with the only other employee, a total fall down drunk named Kelly. After Mike made the formal introductions, he realized that they had forgotten the tools so Mike and Kelly went to get some tools and would return promptly. Before leaving, Mike said that a guy would be dropping off a big piece of equipment for the job and he told me where the equipment should be placed. No sooner had Mike and Kelly left than this huge truck and trailer pull up with a huge excavator and a fancy dude in a shiny pick up truck. I told the big rig driver where to place the excavator and the dude in the shiny truck says I need Mike Enwright to sign this purchase and sale agreement for the machine. I told the man that Mike had to go get some additional tools. The guy was really angry because he was not supposed to leave the machine without the signed agreement but the excavator was off the trailer and I seemed like a nice 16 year old kid. So off they went, the truck and trailer and the dude with the shiny truck.

Once they turned the corner, I ran to that excavator and started it up and pushed every lever and pedal it had. I went forward and backward and swung the boom arm and etc. The biggest part I learned about this machine is that there is a throttle that you need to really rev up the engine to about 3,500 rpms which was slightly over the recommended break in conditions.

When I was comfortable that I ruled that machine and had not damaged anything, I turned it off and sat down on my new toy waiting for Mike and Kelly to return. Who should happen by but a good friend Mike McGarity. I was so excited to tell Mike that I could totally run this fine machine, to wit he said that I could not. That was a challenge that I could not let go unmet. I said fine, you stand at the very end of the boom extension and if I hit you with the bucket I win. So needless to say, I hopped into the excavator and brought the machine up to 4,000 rpms, well above the recommended break in condition, but damn it I had to prove myself. As I was swinging the boom as hard as I could trying to hit/crush my friend Mike, Mr. Enwright turned the corner and came to a screeching halt. He jumped out of the truck and yelled at the top of his lungs "they actually delivered the machine." He didn't care one bit that I was trying to hit/crush my friend.

Day 2- coming soon stay tuned for more.

Written May 10, 2010 3:29pm

Friday 5/7/2010 was a big day. Terri and I had 3 doctor appointments.

Radiology- We met with some of the finest radiologists in Boston; Dr. Weiss, Dr. Kelly and a new Doctor with Training wheels- a nice young man and a great radiation nurse, Sheila Connolly. These folks walked us through the radiation treatment which consists of at least 6 weeks, 5 days per week. The actual treatment is only about 10-15 minutes. Getting to the Brigham and Women's hospital from Duxbury (which I call Dorksbury) is a PITA but its like the L'Oreal commercial…it's expensive, but I am worth it. I have had so many people offer to help with the driving, it's great. I am concerned about Terri, but her response was "how about the poor people that make this drive week in and week out, year in and year out? It's no big deal." My wife is an angel of the highest order.

Mask fitting- For the uninitiated, prior to radiation you need to have a specialized mask made of your face. It was a fun experience. I imagine it's like getting a facial really. These two really nice young ladies had me lay on a table and placed a warm damp mesh material over my face and formed it to my head perfectly. It's sort of like a tight fitting goalie mask. Next they actually buckle it down onto the table. The reason is that since they are going to deliver radiation through a 3 dimensional beam to my head it needs to be precisely located every time otherwise they could unintentionally knock out one of my super powers, i.e. sense of humor or being invisible to pretty women other than my wife.

MRI- last appointment for the day, I needed another MRI to establish a base line for the radiation treatment.

John's Ideal day

If I could spend a day with anyone, I would spend ½ of a day with a great physicist, ½ of a day with Socrates and the third half of the day would be with John Stewart from the Daily Show with a shout out to Click & Clack The Tap It brothers from public radio.

And now more tales from the Crypt:

Preamble to day 2

I walked the 3 miles home from my first hard day of work. It was tiring trying to hit/crush my friend and hook up sewerage for the fine people of Knollwood Rd. While sitting at the dinner table I asked my dad what the story was with that fall down drunken Kelly. My dad said "back in the day, Kelly was actually really smart and the TOP NATIONAL SALESMAN at an industrial company." I said "then what happened?" In my father's typical Boson's mate response he said "a whiskey glass and a woman's ass will make a horse's ass out of you". Now, I had just turned 16 and had no idea what that meant so I said again "what happened?" My dad said "don't be so stupid, it was the booze". Kelly had fallen hard; he lived in a weekly boarding house for salesmen or other people.

My dad's final words about Kelly were "watch him carefully, he has two conditions, either drunk or really drunk, so always keep your eyes open and never let Kelly drive a vehicle. He permanently lost his license a few years ago but I have seen him driving around town."

Day 2-

I show up at 8:00 and Mike and Kelly show around 9. This time they are towing a gas powered portable cement mixer. Mike backs the mixer into position and says "let's unhook it from the tow hitch."

At 16 years old, with 3 years of football, 3 years of track filed along with one year of wrestling behind me, I am in good condition. I'm almost herculean in my mind, so I bend over to lift the cement mixer off the hitch and I cannot move it one bit. I almost got a hernia with that effort. My first thought was, "why am I so weak?" I decided to hop onto the cement mixer and see if there is water or something inside the barrel of the mixer that could possibly make the mixer so heavy. Well guess what? Apparently the last time Mike and Kelly had a job requiring a cement mixer someone forgot to empty the mixer!!!!! So needless to say, we had a cement mixer completely filled with hardened cement.

It took the three of us to lift that mixer up 3 inches to get it off the hitch. Mike Enwright, president, CEO and chairman of Mike Enwright constructions says in a straight face, "this looks bad, but I have seen worse. I know exactly what to do. John, you take this 10 pound sledge hammer and start banging on the side of the cement mixer to break up any loose cement, and I will take Kelly and get an air compressor jack hammer with a bull nose point to use on the inside to break up the residual cement."

So Mike and Kelly hop into the pickup and away they go, leaving me with a 10 pound sledge hammer, a cement mixer and the excavator.

What would any normal 16 year old boy do? Naturally I ran over to the excavator and tried to start it up but alas, Mike was concerned that the owner of the machine might try to come back for it so he took the keys. So my next option was to start breaking up the cement by banging on the wall of the mixer barrel. Guess what? The Boston Big Dig should have been built with this cement; in fact I banged as hard as I could for about 30 minutes and all I got was an ear ache from the mixer echo.

About 2 hours later and after a few beers I am sure, the dream team showed up with an air compressor and a jack hammer. We get the compressor running and hooked up the jack hammer with a bull point bit.

We adjusted the barrel of the mixer from straight up to approximately horizontal so we could stand on the ground, place the bull point into the mixer and "drill baby drill". We were working with an old school jack hammer. I would say it weighed somewhere between 75-90 pounds, so it was a two man job, right? Mike Enwright decided he needed more tools and he left Kelly with me to handle this little job.

Based on my dad's earlier advice never to trust Kelly, we came to the decision that I should handle the Jack hammer and he should sit on his butt in the shade.

The jack hammering began. I had to stop immediately because of two things. The echo was deafening, so I stuffed my ears with old rags. The dust flying out of the machine made it impossible to see and breathe, so I created a complete face mask that allowed me to breathe and not have dust blowing directly into my face. All the time Kelly was watching my struggle while he sat back and sipped on a flask of booze. It just made me so mad. I said to hell with him, put on my full mask, put the bull point into the cement mixer and began the jack hammering process. The more I thought about the whole situation, the more I pressed on, harder and more determined than ever to break all of the cement out and make this machine perfect again.

There was only one small problem; without someone to help me I kept on jack hammering through the cement and through the cement mixer entirely. If there is one thing I learned that day it's that once you puncture a cement mixer the puncturing tool is not easily removed from the hole.

It took an hour for me to finally knock the bull point out of the hole and the rest of the day to gingerly knock out the rest of the cement and to pound the material around the hole together so it sort of worked, except each time the mixer rotated it would shoot about a pound of cement onto whoever stood in the line of fire. Mike arrived and I told him about the incident, His response was, "it's not mine; I just borrowed it from a friend". Mike really never got mad. Besides, I was the only one working as Kelly was passed out under a maple tree.

Day 3

 Coming soon so stay tuned

Written May 14, 2010 5:24pm

Hey all,

Its John. It's been a busy week and I wanted to be able to give you all a concise report.

Tuesday 5/11- appointment with the oncologist for clinical trial final approval and review my chemo regime. The exam went really well, in fact I scored 100%. It was an interesting exercise. So, pending a final blood draw, I am in.

Thursday 5/13- appointment with radiation oncology for final mask fitting. If you go to the welcome spot on this website you will get a larger picture of the mask. Starting Tuesday 5/18, I will have 6 weeks, 5 days/week of radiation.

A great thing about the Brigham and Women's, Dana Farber and Harvard University partnership is that together they have all of the latest and greatest tools. The radiation machine I am laying on is the newest in the industry with 5 beams of radiation, meaning there is very precise control. I am really glad that the fall down drunken Kelly is not running this machine as you will see later in day 3- tales from the crypt.

I am very excited to get going on this whole thing, so it's off this weekend and away we go on Tuesday.

I would like to give a shout out to my brother Charlie who just completed his final chemo treatment on Wednesday. He has been going into Mass General Hospital for extensive treatment since January. So congratulations!!!!!!!!

I would also like to give a shout out to Kal Akal who recently suffered some heart issues and is on the mend. Kal is the Innova plant manager. When I spoke to him one of the first things I said was, "why can't I have my own drama without sharing the spot light?" He is at home and resting.

Day 3-

On my 3 mile walk to work, I started to think that I was beginning to get the hang of the job. Mike Enwright, president and CEO always arrived late, and Mike always found a way to leave when there was work to do. Kelly was always either drunk or very drunk.

Today was different. When I arrived on the job, I learned that Mike and Kelly could arrive on time. I also learned that Mike Enwright did not know the difference between water proof and non water proof markers because it had rained and the Mike Enwright sign had bled away to a Rorschach test ink blot.

Up to now we actually did not do much. In fact, today was the first day that we were going to break ground and connect the fine people of Knollwood Rd. with their much needed sewer line. To my great surprise, who do you think was starting up the excavator? It was

Kelly, yes Kelly. Apparently due to some legal loop hole, even though he was banned from driving a car for life, he could still keep his hydraulic operator's license. My first thoughts were "god save me" and "stay as far away as possible from the machine".

To give Kelly credit, I think he tried a night off the booze and showed up sober with a massive hangover and a serious case of the shakes, to the point where his fine motor control was out of control. When he tried to maneuver the controls he would shake so badly that it would affect the excavator hydraulics causing the entire machine to shake, which to a 16 year old kid was funny as hell. After Mike saw Kelly trying to operate the machine he said "Kelly you are better a little drunk than sober so why don't you have a little drink before we begin?" So after several huge gulps of Mad Dog 20/20, Kelly was much steadier with hands like a surgeon. He hopped onto the excavator and was ready to go.

Previously an engineer had marked the street with paint to identify the water, electric and other utilities and most of all where the sewer was supposed to go. My job was to use the jack hammer and cut through the black top so there would be a nice clean edge which the excavator could follow if it was anyone other than Kelly. Cutting pavement with a jack hammer is actually fun. The hammer does all the work. After you cut through the pavement, you pull it up and repeat and repeat and repeat and repeat.

After about an hour, I had cut about 50 to 60 feet of pavement, which was enough for Kelly to begin excavating. As it turns out, when Kelly was about half drunk he was a pretty good operator. In no time Kelly had dug a trench about 12-15 feet deep. To hook up to the existing sewer on route 28, we needed to tap into a manhole structure. The procedure is to start digging a few feet away from the structure and clear away as much dirt as possible. Then you send the lowest most expendable person down the trench which was me, of course.

I lowered a ladder that reached the bottom of the trench, while Kelly shut down the machine and had a snort. That actually gave me great comfort knowing that the machine was not going to crush me. Once

I got to the bottom of the trench, I looked up and it seemed like I was down a 100 foot hole. I started digging as quickly as possible trying to find the sewer junction and get the heck out of that hole. While I am digging my heart out, an object came flying out of nowhere and hit me right on the head.

I figure the topside guys are messing with me, but as it turns out, Mike had thrown me the world smallest hard hat, which was the size of a prescription pill bottle cap. He leaned over and said "put this on for protection". As I placed the pill bottle sized hard hat on my melon sized head a new face appeared over the trench. This guy had a real hard hat on and a logo on his hat which said "Massachusetts Department of Safety". The inspector said, "please very carefully get out of the trench and try not to touch the sides of the trench as it looks very unstable". I had noticed earlier that as I was digging there were little bits of rock and debris falling onto me but I thought that was normal. Just as I reached the top of the trench one of the walls let go and filled the trench with about 3-4 feet dirt. If I had been down the hole it would have made for a much longer story.

Once I was on the surface, the inspector said, "son how old are you?" I said proudly," I just turned 16 two weeks ago". I guess that was the wrong answer because I was told that you had to be at least 18 to work on this type of job site, so I was immediately terminated. Mike Enwright construction got a hefty fine and the dude with the shiny pickup truck finally showed up with his purchase and sale agreement ready for Mike's signature.

Needless to say, the inspector shut down the job site. The good people of Knollwood Road would have to wait another year for their sewerage connection.

As Mike and Kelly broke for lunch and drove away in the Rorschach test vehicle which was headed the same way I was walking, Mike yelled to me, "don't worry, I will give your paycheck to your dad".

I was pissed off for a bunch of reasons. I understood the law, but I could not understand how those two clowns could just leave me there when we were heading in the same direction. So as I trudged the 3 miles home, who did I meet but my old friend Mike McGarity who I was trying to hit/crush earlier in the story. After we talked for a while, I started to feel better and better and realized what a crazy story I had to tell.

After telling Mike how badly I needed a job to make some money, he said the place he worked at was hiring and that I should get cleaned up and apply today. So with some new pep in my step and glide in my stride I went home, took a bath and headed off to my new destiny.

Day 4- stay tuned for more.

Written May 19, 2010 7:58pm

Hey all its John,

I hope you all are well; it's been a while since I posted but I wanted to wait until we had more information.

Warning – there is some language that may be upsetting (vulgar) however I am sure its nothing you all have not heard or used in the last 2 weeks. In fact a lot of you folks use this language as regular or only means of communication. I certainly do.

Tuesday 5/18- It's my first day of chemo AKA TMZ, radiation (AKA Linear Accelerator or LA) and trial drug (AKA HCQ). Naturally I am a little nervous, given that the reported side effects, though rare, are pretty scary. We arrive about noon for a blood draw. I have been stuck with so many needles that this is nothing, although they take a lot of tubes, usually in the 4-6 range. I always show up enthusiastic for the blood draw and place my arm on the board but it's my veins that are chicken. I swear that when I am having blood work done all of my veins somehow bury themselves down deep and say something like " I was stuck last time, let one of the other veins get stuck or how about using the other arm. Those veins never get stuck, it's just not fair".

Next we meet with the oncology nurse and the clinical trial coordinator, Stephen. These folks are the best; they are really doing god's work. I like Stephen a lot. In fact I told him that I had a few openings for a new favorite nephew and he was down with that. My big question to the nurse was correct dosage amounts. Here is my reasoning and concern. The brain is largely made of fatty type tissue. The drugs therefore must be able to pass through the blood brain barrier and be fat soluble. My concern was that since my ideal body weight is approximately 190 pounds but my actual body weight is 254 pounds, my thinking was that with all that extra, shall we say, adipose tissue, the chemo chemical might be more attracted to the local adipose tissue rather than the brain area. Nurse Debra was cool and she said that yes that would be a concern if I was morbidly obese, so since I am just obese (my words, not hers), we are good. We spend most of the appointment reviewing the drugs and the routine to take the drugs.

The HCQ needs to be taken 2 X per day with food at least 6 hours apart and the TMZ is taken once a day on an empty stomach ideally 2 hours before the radiation for optimum effectiveness. There is an anti nausea medicine called Zofran which is taken at least an hour before the TMZ.

In a nut shell yesterday to get all of the doses in I had to eat breakfast and start fasting by 10:30 am and did not eat again until around 6:00, but since I am obese it was not too hard. I took my first HCQ with dinner and had to stay up until midnight to eat another meal so I could have the second HCQ. Then up at 5 am to eat again and go back to the hospital fasting so I could take my TMZ but I had to remember to take my anti Nausea pill at 7:30am so I would not be sick.

My point for writing about this is that it's really hard to keep track of everything and I would say almost impossible for an elderly person without help. If you know someone going through this kind of situation, please reach out and ask them if they need some help because it is truly overwhelming for an obese guy with an incredible wife to keep track of all of the details.

The next appointment was with the Dr. and Stephen again for asking questions and such. I had one burning question that was based on hopeful information I had received but was too afraid to follow up on because I was also afraid it would be followed up with some bad news which I was not prepared to hear.

I asked the doctor straight out, "what about the tumor"? His response was that there is no tumor left and that the last MRI did not show any evidence of tumor. Naturally this is very good news, to wit, I said, "so the radiation, chemo and clinical trial are essentially a mop up operation to kill any little fuckers left behind?" The Dr. says, "did you just use the word fuckers?" I said, "yes I did". His response was, "that is a great word. I just don't get to use it around here and since I have a two year old it would not be cool to have a two year old running around the house saying "fucker, fucker"." Needless to say my doctor is cool, intelligent and able to communicate to anyone at any level (even able to get down to mine on occasion); truly an amazing person.

Finally the treatment- due to all kinds of hitches and snags I finally got called to the LA at about 3:30. I was pumped to finally get going. I hopped onto the table and the face mask got locked down. I swear either that mask shrunk over the weekend or my face gained weight because it was extremely tight. Everyone leaves the room and the machine begins its cycle which is supposed to last about 10-12 minutes. The machine is kind of like an alien robot with a camera that floats over your head and goes from one side of your head to the other with this bright light kind of like "Close Encounters of the Third Kind" and there is a sort of soft noise. All of sudden the machine stops and the technician comes over and says the machine broke down. It will be 5 minutes. Can you wait or do you want to get out of the mask? I am thinking anyone can wait 5 extra minutes so I opted to stay locked down. What a huge mistake because now 5 minutes turns into 10 then 20 then 30 minutes. By now I am beginning to panic because I am locked in and nobody is around. Thank goodness for deep breathing exercises because I was able to manage my panic and get through the rest of the radiation. When I finally got off the machine I had two headaches, one where the tumor was and a 2nd dead center between my frontal lobes, along with a mild tooth ache and blurred vision in my right eye. Good times!

Thankfully all of the symptoms decreased over night; however I discussed them with the radiologist the next day. My concern was that since radiation is cumulative would these symptoms get worse. I was afraid that may head might explode or something. His response was that typically these reactions actually decrease over several days. The doctor was correct, because today 5/19 I had my 2nd radiation and it went really well with no side effects.

Day 4- I promise to get that posted ASAP, radiation makes me very tired.

Written May 20, 2010 7:13pm

Hey all its John again,

First, a radiation update then funny tales from the crypt- day 4 preamble

As I have mentioned many times before, the good folks at the DF and B&W are amazing. They are able to smile and help the people with the most unfathomable conditions. These institutions are really worthy of our support.

Radiation was a breeze. Terri and I showed up about 15 minutes ahead of schedule and they took me right on time. I hopped onto the table and said a quick hello to the alien robot, got locked down and it was done in about 12 minutes. Actually they played Elton John's Tiny Dancer over the loud speaker, (I thought Elton was singing about me) and part of one other tune and it was a wrap. None of the first day side effects.

Medication- We have had some trouble with getting our insurance carrier to approve the TMZ. It is quite expensive so I understand their reticence. I was approved for one pill at a time to be dispensed at the DF infusion clinic which required us to head into Boston at least 2 hours ahead of the scheduled radiation, so we have had to leave the house at 6:30 for a 10:30 appointment. Obviously this is unacceptable. Thanks to our doctor and his talented staff who called our insurance company about every 2 hours. Yesterday I decided to call out the big guns. I asked my boss to get involved along with his assistant Mary, which is roughly equal to releasing a hive of African bees at a nudist colony. They are persistent and know how to get things done (a big thank you). We finally got approval for 7 of these pills which hopefully will take us to a point where the insurance company has finally reviewed and approved the dispersal of the TMZ pills which is the standard of care for treatment. The point of dragging you all through this drama is that you should not accept the insurance company BS. You need to advocate for yourself and don't be afraid to enlist others to help you. Thank goodness I have a wonderful support network at Innova and at the Dana Farber or this ordeal would be so much worse.

Remember there are only 3 types of people in the world:
Those who make things happen
Those who watch things happen
Those who wonder, what the hell happened?

Now funny tales from the crypt

Prelude to day 4

After getting the bounce from Mike Enwright construction, I met Mike McGarity and filled him in on my unceremonious departure from the construction/sewer industry. Mike was great. He said that he had a great job at Star Market in the Redstone shopping center in Stoneham, which was only about 6 miles away. They were hiring carriage wranglers. Mike was working that afternoon at 3 pm and if I could get to his house, he would be happy to help me land my new dream job. I practically ran the 3 miles home to jump into the tub and head off to Mike's house.

Once I was all cleaned up, I put on my best pair of yellow checkered bell bottom pants and cool shirt. I was just about to hop on my bike when my mother asked where I was going. I told her about the carriage wrangling job and to her credit she realized immediately how far the Star Market was away from home and she said "I hope you get the job. We will find a way to get you back and forth". My parents were bombastic in so many ways but they always supported me when I needed it.

Since we only had one car and my dad walked to work, my mom was able to drive me and my cool yellow checkered bell bottoms to Mike's house. Mike had his license, so he drove us to the Star Market. He showed me where to apply. I filled out the job application and Mike was nice enough to bring the hiring supervisor over to interview me. The cashier supervisor's name was Tommy Walsh. He was old; I pegged him at 20-22 years old. How could anyone get that much responsibility without putting in a lot of years? Tommy was a nice guy. He wore a white coat with a tie. You can always tell management because of the ties and white coats.

The interview was really short. Tommy was looking for someone that could wrangle carriages from the entire parking lot which was about 2-3 acres, as there were at least 10 other stores in the plaza. After about 10 minutes of small talk Tommy said "I need a guy that can wrangle carriages in any weather, doesn't call in sick and will work Friday and Saturday nights." I said "I am your man for this job". He said "great. Tomorrow is Friday. You will be working 4-8 pm. For god sakes, don't ever wear those pants to work. They are awful." I must admit that I was taken aback by Tommy's total lack of taste in clothing. After all, what's cooler than yellow checkered bell bottoms?

I had landed my second job in one week! I was walking on air, which was a good thing because I now had to walk 6 miles home, since Mike was still working. As I got closer to home I started thinking of short cuts that would save time. This was especially important since my Bosun mate father had a schedule just like the Navy. He arrived home every night at 4:35 and dinner was on the table at 5:00 sharp. If anything disturbed this ritual, it was grounds for keel hauling (those of you who know my dad from the old days will totally agree; he only got nice in his old age). It was about 4:30 and I was about 2 miles from home so I took a gamble to save some time. The only hitch was I had to jump over a couple of 6 foot fences and cross onto private industrial property that had a security guard. I decided I would rather face a security guard than my father having dinner at 5:10 rather than 5:00.

I reached the fence, put my shoes into the fence, climbed up and over I went without a hitch, but my luck had run out. The security guard, who drank with Kelly, was having a sober moment. He saw me and started to chase. Naturally I started running and got to the second fence. I put my shoes into the fence and up and over I went except that one of my bell bottoms caught on the fence. I was able to land on my feet but one leg of my coolest pair of pants was now shredded. This tragic event did not faze me because I had a new job that paid $1.35/hour so I could buy more pants. Besides I could make them into cool shorts and I was going to be home by 4:59 so dinner could be served on time.

.

As we sat down to dinner, my father already knew about me losing my first job due to the age situation. He was unaware about my new job and I was excited to fill him in on it. His first words were, "how the hell are you going to get back and forth?" My mother was excellent at managing my father. She said, "Bob, it's important that Johnny gets a job and we will support him." The old man was pissed off. He looked at me sideways the entire meal because he knew that he might be the chief bosons mate but the admiral had spoken.

Written Jun 3, 2010 7:34pm

Hi all, its John,

Sorry it's been so long since my last post. Since beginning radiation, chemo and the trial drug, my energy has fallen almost as fast as my hair. Let's face it; I did not have much to start with but all of a sudden it's like oak leaves in October. All of the leaves are falling at the same time.

Well we have completed 40% of the radiation sessions. I say we because Terri has been driving from Duxbury to the B&W hospital every day. Needless to say, it's a hassle but waiting in radiation we met folks from Chicago and Fort Meyers that thought it was worth the trip, along with folks from all over the USA and abroad.

We met with the Chemo and Radiation Doctors this week. They both asked the same questions. "How are you feeling?" Actually I feel pretty good, except I am very tired. In fact, I have been taking 2 hour afternoon naps every day to regain some strength. It's kind of like every day is Saturday. A great friend of mine, Steve Torrey, has made the drive to Boston during rush hour. It's really special. I don't know how people can do this daily. The commute is actually worse than the radiation treatments, if that's possible.

Funny tales from the Crypt

Day 4

I was so pumped for my first shift as a carriage wrangler, I wore my second favorite pair of pants. They were powder blue with brown checks; not as cool as yellow but still very fashionable. Since Mike Mcgarity had to work at 3 and I had to work at 4, it made sense for me to ride my bike to Mike's house and catch a 3 o'clock ride to work. Back in the day, a 16 year old kid riding a bike was totally uncool. In fact the normal 3 mile ride to Mike's turned into almost 5 miles because I had to avoid any potentially cool areas where my uncoolness might be spotted, even though I was wearing very cool pants. By the time I got to Mike's, I realized that my chain guard was missing, so my remaining cool pair of pants was pretty well greased up on the right leg. Sadly, powder blue pants show the grease pretty well. In any event, I arrived at Mike's. We jumped into the car and drove to the store. I tried to clock in early but Tommy was right there to say "you cannot start at 3pm, you start at 4pm, otherwise I would have to give you a 15 minute paid break."

I asked about getting some job training, setting goals and measuring progress. Only kidding.

Tommy said "why don't you go over to the drug store and get a soda or something and we will see you at 4 pm sharp." Waiting to start my new career was so exciting. The drug store was all the way over on the other side of the parking lot. I did go all the way over to the drug store for a soda. While on my way over to the drug store I noticed how many carriages were strewn in the furthest reaches of the lot.

Once I finally punched my card, I sought out Tommy to tell him about the far away carriages. He said, "Go for it. Nobody ever gets those unless I yell at the other wranglers". I had found my niche. I would travel the perimeter of the lot looking for wayward carriages, make a carriage train and start pushing for home. Since football started in less than a month, I used this opportunity to build enormous carriage trains. My rationale was that this would be a good chance to build my legs and stamina. After a while Tommy noticed that there were too many carriages to fit in the storage area so he asked me to start bagging groceries. My first shift and already I am promoted to bagging groceries! This was a meteoric rise, although my bagging promotion was short lived. Tommy really did not give me any bagging instructions like "don't put the gallon of milk on top of the bread", "don't put raw meat on top of the veggies" and my favorite, "eggs break easily". So needless to say, I made quite a few boo boos before Tommy called me over to give me some words of encouragement. As I recall he said "what the hell is wrong with you, don't you know that milk crushes bread?" I answered honestly "no, this is my first day of bagging groceries".

Tommy was a good guy and he looked so cool with his white jacket and tie. He took me aside and explained the basics of bagging, and his last words were that I should start over and remember to move around to the busiest cashiers so people can get going as quickly as possible. I felt good about myself and I did a great job of properly bagging groceries and moving from cashier to cashier for a while. I moved like a hummingbird from cashier to cashier. I was on fire until one cashier, her name was Martha, started talking to me. Yes, actually I was 16 and never really had a conversation with a girl that was not a blood relative. Martha and I had the most wonderful conversation about where we lived, how many siblings we each had and our favorite colors. I had no idea that girls could have conversations. I was spell bound until two things happened. First she told me she was going into 12th grade (an older woman) and second this guy wearing a suit and tie came up to me and said " go over and start bagging at another cashier". To wit I said "who the hell are you?" He replied "I am the store manager, if you want your job you better move it now. Where the hell is Tommy?"

As it turns out, Tommy was outside smoking a butt along with some of the cashiers, a practice that the store manager frowned upon. So not only was I in trouble but I got Tommy in trouble too. You see while I was focused on Martha's brilliant conversation all of the other lines backed up because Martha had placed a closed sign on the belt which I did not notice.

I knew when Tommy was mad because the tips of his ears turned red. When he approached me his ears were completely crimson. I had really messed up. Tommy pulled me aside and said, "thanks a lot, because of you I have to work Saturday nights now. I have been trying to get off on Saturday nights for 2 years, and since you are working tomorrow night I will have a special job for you." I was so excited because I just loved special jobs; they are always so different and challenging.

After all that excitement, I almost forgot it was quitting time and Mike was waiting in his car. On my way out the door Martha stopped me and asked if I was working tomorrow and I proudly said yes and I would be on a special job! Mike drove me home after swinging by his house to pick up my bike. I asked him if he was working tomorrow and he said no, so you are on your own. I had an immediate sinking feeling because I would need to ask my folks for a ride to and from work, gulp!

Day 5 coming soon

Written Jun 14, 2010 4:35pm

Hey all,

It's John. Sorry its been so long between updates. First, I would like to thank everyone so much for all of the cards, letters, prayers, gifts and etc. I would like to especially like to thank Mike Falsone for agreeing to buy me a 2011 Mecedes AMG with all of the bells and whistles.

Medical Update

There is not a lot to say except that radiation, chemo and the drug trial have taken a huge toll on my body, mind and hair, which I did not have any to spare in the first place. I won't make this into a crying session but fatigue and severe vertigo have knocked me down but I am not out! As I told my oncologist, it feels like he is taking me as close to death as possible without actually killing me (hopefully).

Medical Insurance- I cannot over emphasize how important this is for everyone to have. Please make this a priority for yourself, friends, relatives and etc. I want to give you a real example. I just got the bill for the original surgery. It was enormous, but after BCBS negotiated a 45% discount it was just big. I have been reviewing all of the charges and BCBS has really done a good job of negotiating. I cannot imagine if I did not have insurance and with no negotiating power what the damages would be. I was in great health until April 2010. If this can happen to me, it can happen to anyone.

tales from the crypt

Day 5- coming soon, actually I am too tired to write anymore today. Sorry.
J

Written Jul 17, 2010 1:10pm

Hi all,

It's John. I am sorry that it has taken me so long to get back to the web site. I must be a Catholic because it has been 33 days since my last posting.

Thanks to all for all of your cards, letters and calls. I feel all of the positive energy and prayers. Please keep them coming.

I will give you a quick recap of chemo and radiation- it sucks!

Nobody wants to hear about side effects so I won't go into it. Suffice to say that over the last 8 weeks I have met with the following:

radiation-oncologist
neuro-oncologist
neurosurgeon
ear nose and throat doctor
Opthamologist
rheumatologist

All to confirm that I was having nasty side effects. The winner of the most alarming statement is: "Never seen that before".

I have been off of radiation and chemo for 18 days and am now feeling so much better. I naively thought that day 1 post radiation I would feel better, but the effects seemed to accumulate for about a week. Anyhow, that is becoming a memory in the rear view mirror.

While going through this process, some of our neighbors did some wonderful things for us.

1. John C. and Rick F. stopped by while heading to the dump and asked "what do you have to get rid of?"
2. Doug and Pam W. weeded our yard while we were away. Such a blessing.

3. Rick and Cindy F. stopped by daily to take our year old labrador Tessie, AKA large Marge, for a walk and a swim.

While these folks offered to do these chores and more; we would have never asked them in a million years. Perhaps there is someone out there you know that would also benefit from a sneak attack of kindness. It meant so much to Terri and me.

From all of the people that I have seen, most people say I look fantastic. I take this to mean either I really looked terrible before all of this or their expectation was that I would look like an old catcher's mitt. So when you see me for the first time, please just say "John, you look as ugly as ever".

I promise to write soon with tales from the crypt.

Written Aug 17, 2010 7:23am

Hi,

Well, it's been a crazy few weeks.

John is in the hospital (Brigham & Women's) after emergency surgery late Sunday night, or rather early Monday morning, for a perforated colon. We don't have answers yet as to why this happened, but it could be totally unrelated to his cancer. He's recovering nicely, but will be in the hospital for 5-7 days, and then have the usual recovery time from surgery to deal with.

This was actually the 4th trip to an emergency room since June! Twice for seizures, once for severe joint pain, and now this. We are becoming all too familiar with hospitals, doctors, nurses, procedures etc.

Anyway, he's trying his best to make his doctors and nurses laugh, so you know he's doing ok.

It's been a tough week for the Nickersons all around, as John's brother, (Chickie to us, Charlie to others) is back in the hospital for treatment of his non-Hodgkins Lymphoma. We are all praying for a full cure for both Nickerson brothers.

Jamie will be coming from Chicago later this week, on a scheduled vacation, so we are really looking forward to having her here.

Written Sep 12, 2010 8:46am

Hi all,

It's John. I am sorry it's been so long since my last post. As you can see I have had some challenges. The latest is shingles. Everyone says shingles are painful and I can agree they are something special. I cannot overemphasize how important it is to get symptoms checked out as soon as possible. The one thing I have learned throughout this mid life tune up is to act quickly when something is not right. Don't let things go without follow-up! Fortunately, the shingles incident was diagnosed early, so I did not have to go through the worst of the outbreak.

I want to thank everyone so much for all of your cards, prayers, good wishes and visits. They cheer me up beyond measure. Sadly, I have not been in a position to say thank you sooner. Kathy L. sent some Dilbert cartoons that really hit the spot. Thank you all so much for keeping me in your prayers and thoughts. I can feel the energy. Please, please, please keep them coming!

I really don't have too much funny stuff going on right now except that I keep threatening to make my 24 stomach staples into a nice necklace or bracelet.

I am getting stronger every day; as a result my off beat sense of humor is returning. A quick exit story from the hospital.

As an Irish Catholic, I was brought up to be modest, actually extremely modest. Everyone in my family and neighborhood was brought up in the same fashion. Over the years my hyper-modesty has worn down a bit but I am still "old school". I was recently discharged from the hospital for stomach surgery. I was wearing the infamous hospital johnny i.e. closed in the front and open in the back. I find the wide open back unacceptable (especially without underwear), so I came up with the two johnny system where one johnny goes in front and a second johnny is put on the back so technically I am covered from all angles.

The two johnny system maintains modesty for most situations. The only weakness is sitting in a wheel chair. I had identified this weakness and got a blanket for my lap to maintain my modesty given that I was not able to wear underwear during my hospital stay.

I was so happy to be discharged and have all of the tubes and needles removed and just get home to finally start the healing process. As planned, Terri got the wheel chair. I got into the chair, placed the blanket on my lap and away we went. We were on the 8th floor, had to travel down long corridors passing countless people on the way to the valet parking. Upon arrival at the valet parking area, a sweet little old lady came up to me and said, "sir would you mind if I covered you up? You are exposed." In our haste to get out of the hospital, while rolling along in the wheel chair, a gentle breeze had blown my 2 johnny system and blanket up to an obscene level. So much for hospital modesty. That was the first good laugh I had in a long time. I did get an email application for a nudist colony but I decided to pass on that.

I am training for the three mile brain tumor walk on 10/2. Already I am up to about 1.4 miles and trying to add about a tenth of a mile per day. Sadly, prior to the second surgery, I was walking almost 3.5 miles per day.

Written Sep 24, 2010 10:14am

Quick update...

John was finally able to go back on his chemotherapy last Thursday. 5 days on, 23 days off, for 10 more cycles after this one. He handled it like a champ, with fatigue being the major side effect. This cycle was delayed by about 3 weeks because of the recent surgery, so I'm relieved that he's back on plan.

We had a really great visit with all of John's work colleagues. It was wonderful to meet everyone after all of these years, and to put the faces with the names. Everyone was so kind and welcoming, and I now feel like I'm part of the Innova team. And if 3 hour lunches are routine, I'm in!

John continues to recuperate after his last surgery, and is feeling much stronger. We're walking whenever he feels up to it, to try to build up his stamina for the brain tumor walk that we are doing next week.

Thank you for all of your cards, calls and emails. We really appreciate your prayers and thoughts. John's feeling well enough to be a little bored, so feel free to call and say hello.

Terri

Written Sep 30, 2010 6:22pm

Hi all, it's John,

I hope you all are well. Sorry it's been so long since my last update. First a health update and then some funny stuff from the crypt – day 5 at Star Market.

Medical Update

Overall things are getting better all of the time. I am regaining my strength and looking forward to returning to work.

This week I met with Dr. Askari. He is the general surgeon that is following my progress after the emergency stomach surgery. I like him a lot except he wears a NY Yankees hat and has a Yankees ID holder; otherwise he is excellent. In fact, I do not need to see him again for six months, so that is a really bright spot.

We also met with Doctors Weiss and Kelly. These are the radiation oncologists that managed my radiation. The results from my last MRI were that the tumor region has slightly enlarged but that is consistent with a condition called "pseudo progression". Pseudo progression results from the combination of radiation and chemo. The cells around the former tumor site are really irritated and are dying off with resultant swelling. Naturally whenever a tumor site changes there is concern. One really good piece of information is that the enlarged area does not have an increased blood supply which indicates that the change is not related to tumor activity.

Dr. Norden said that generally patients with pseudo progression have a better outcome which makes sense considering that it shows a higher sensitivity to the treatment.

One part of the appointment I enjoy is the neurological exam. The exam consists of simple tasks such as touching your nose with your finger, walking heel to toe (aka sobriety test) and a general strength test. The last part of the exam consists of the doctor placing two fingers into my hands and asking me to squeeze them as hard as I can. I always ask the doctor "do you really want me to squeeze as hard as I can?" When they say yes, then I apply as much pressure as possible and enjoy hearing them beg for mercy. Naturally Terri pointed out that I should not be squeezing too hard because neurosurgeons need their hands to operate and we might be liable for any injury.

Funny tales from the Crypt-
Day 5

I recommend that you refresh the story by rereading Day 4.

Day 5

A summer Saturday morning, generally a happy time, extra sleep and no pressure, except this Saturday I had to summon the courage to ask my parents for a ride to and from work. For a normal family this would be no big deal i.e. a ride to work at 3 pm and a return ride at 9:30 pm, total distance less than 6 or 7 miles each way, total time required less than 20 minutes. In my family this type of request was treated like I asked my parents to climb Mt. Everest with an elephant on their backs in Bermuda shorts.

My strategy for dealing with special requests was developed over time and was fool proof. In a nutshell, get up and complete my chores without being told. I got up, ate a quick breakfast, mowed the lawn, weeded the garden and the flower beds then asked if anything else needed to be done. Since Saturday was shopping day, I waited for their return so I could rush out and start unloading the car and told my folks to go inside and I would bring all the groceries in.

Now the trap is set. As we sat down for lunch I casually mentioned that I was working tonight, to wit my father in his typical gruff voice said "how are you going to get to work'? I replied that I was going to ride my bike. I knew that the next words would be from my mother who said "Bob, look at all the work Johnny did today, we cannot let him ride his bike that late at night". At that point I wanted to yell "YAHTZEE" but did not because while I would get my ride I also knew the old man was pissed.

Needless to say I spent the rest of the day laying low and keeping out of my father's sight. At 2:30 I reminded my father about the ride I needed. He grumbled and said "get in the car" so off we went. We hit about five minutes worth of traffic and my dad moaned and groaned like he was giving birth to a cow. As he let me out of the car his last words were "you better be in the parking lot at 9:30 sharp or you'll be walking home".

God, I could not wait to get out of that car, I was so afraid someone would see me. As I was walking into the store another cart wrangler saw me and asked if that was my dad? I said "no, I hitchhiked to work and that kindly old man picked me up and dropped me at the door".

Tommy was the first person I saw when I got into the store. He still blamed me for having to work Saturday nights. His only words were "clock in, get to work and come see me at 8:30 and stay away from Martha. You two are trouble".

The next person I met was Martha who said "come bag for me. We can talk about the party my cousin Gerry is having tonight". I told her what Tommy said and said we would need to be really careful given Tommy's pissed off state plus my dad was going to pick me up at 9:30 sharp. Martha said "don't worry. Gerry has a car and he'd be happy to drive you home after the party". My mind went into overdrive. How could I tell the old man that I did not need a ride because I was going to a party? What was my special Tommy task? Did Martha really think I was cool?

At 8:30 I reported to Tommy who led me to the back of the store to the poultry storage area, which was a refrigerated area where the fresh chicken were stored. On Saturday nights, the room got cleaned. This meant taking everything out (tonight there were two pallets of whole chickens, 24 cartons to a pallet) washing and sanitizing the room, putting fresh ice into each box and putting the pallets back into the room. Tommy said that normally this is a two man job but I was such a go getter I could do this all myself. I like a challenge so I got started immediately. It took me about 5 minutes to realize that I was in trouble because this was a really cold wet job and sadly there were no spare boots or gloves available tonight. Regardless, I did the best I could although my hands were freezing and I had lots of chicken juice on my shoes and third coolest pair of powder blue bell bottom pants. I got the job done by 9:15. I began looking for Martha and Gerry to talk about the party and most importantly the ride home. When I finally found them the first words out of their mouths were "you smell like chicken". Gerry confirmed he would give me a ride home so I steeled myself to tell my father that I had a ride home.

At precisely 9:30 the old man appeared like a ghost out of the darkness. I walked to the car and got inside and said "dad I got invited to a party. I will be home early and I am sorry that you had to come all the way over here". I was prepared for a quick smack to the head but my dad just said okay be home by 11:00, you know how your mother likes to lock the house up. She is always afraid of being broken into.

Stupidly I said "dad, we've got the crappiest house in town. Who is going to break into the crappiest house in town"? The reality was my uncle Ralph had the crappiest house in town. He lived next door. We had the 2nd crappiest house in town and my uncle Allen had the 3rd crappiest house in town which was diagonal to our houses. My uncle Allen also had a great dog named Pepe. More about him later.

The last words my dad said were, "be home by 11pm" and "you smell like chicken".

Written Nov 16, 2010 2:12pm

Hi,
I know it's been quite a while since we posted. Mostly that's been because John's been feeling great, and we were just keeping our heads down and getting through the treatments. John has completed 3 of the maintenance rounds of chemo. He did have some seizures since I last posted, but mostly things have been going pretty well.

On Thursday, he had another MRI. This one shows something in the former tumor site and a huge amount of swelling in his brain. It also showed reduced blood flow to the area, which as with the prior MRI's, seemed to indicate that the mass was more likely to be radiation related dead cells than active tumor. However, due to all of the swelling, and also because of the timing, John had a PET scan on Monday, to try to get a better idea of what was going on. The PET scan seemed to indicate tumor growth, although we understand that they are not always reliable.

So, there have been some conflicting signals as to what's going on. The thing that is clear is that there is something in John's brain that is causing a great deal of swelling. He's been lucky that he hasn't had any symptoms yet, and that he feels so good. His doctor thinks that if we continue on the course of treatment that he's been on, he will soon start having symptoms, maybe headaches or vision issues. Both his neuro-oncologist and his neurosurgeon feel that the best thing to do right now is to operate to remove the mass. This should relieve the pressure and reduce the swelling, and will also give them tissue to examine to figure out exactly what's going on. They are confident that he will come through this surgery well, since he did so great after the first one.

While he's recovering from the surgery, his doctor will work out what the next treatment should be. There are some good options, depending on what the pathology report shows.

So, surgery is scheduled for next Monday at Brigham & Women's. Our superstar adopted niece neurosurgeon, Dr. Golby, will be operating, and we have complete faith in her. John is ready to "get 'er done" and is feeling upbeat and confident.

I'll post again when he's out of surgery on Monday.

As always, thanks for all of your support and prayers.

love,
Terri

Written Nov 18, 2010 7:55am

Hi all,

I'ts John. Sorry its been a while since I have updated the web site but I thought I should make a feeble attempt.

As you probably have heard, there is a setback. Cures and treatments for cancer and related diseases are progressing rapidly but the pace needs to increase.

Please remember that every journey of 1,000 miles begins with either a flat tire or a dead battery. That's how I am approaching this new development.

I have had about every test you can have. Due to the limits of the testing protocols, there is no 100% way to determine what is going on. I feel great, however there is swelling that was creating slight headaches, which I would have ignored had I not been sensitized to the danger of headaches no matter how small. As of today I am asymptomatic but that could change at any time so speed it essential.

After meeting with Dr. Norden, Dr. Golby and Terri it was determined that the best path forward is to redo the craniotomy, collect samples and confirm what is going on which could be nothing (no surprise there) or some progression, which will lead to an additional treatment plan.

Additional radiation therapy is not an option. Dr. Golby did say that I could have this operation over and over as needed so I am thinking about getting either a zipper or Velcro.

My hair is growing back. In fact, I was growing one hair 7 inches long to make a lock of love wig donation for some poor bugger but Dr. Golby said she is doing the exact same operation so goodbye wig donation for now. Perhaps someone should contact Tom Brady of the Patriots and ask him to step up in my stead.

Written Nov 30, 2010 9:30am

Hello again,

We just got some great news...

The pathology report came back showing that what was removed was almost entirely dead cells (radiation effect), with very little live tumor cells. Also, the MRI that John had the second night after surgery showed a significant reduction in swelling, so soon after the surgery. So, John's neuro-oncologist, Dr. Norden, wants to continue the treatment that John was on. Sometime next week, he will go back on his chemotherapy treatment (Temodar) 5 days on, 23 days off. He's had 3 of these cycles so far, so I'm assuming he will have at least 9 more, but we'll see.

In any case, we are thrilled and relieved at the results, and pleased that he won't have to switch to some other potentially more difficult treatment.

John continues to feel better every day, and his spirits are great. I'm so proud of him!

Terri

Written Dec 13, 2010 5:07pm

Dear Friends and Family,

It is with so much sadness that we write to let you know that John's brother Charlie (Chickie to old friends and family) passed away today. John looked up to him his whole life, and tells many stories of chasing around after him as a kid.

We already miss him so much and send our love and support to our sister-in-law, Elaine, and to his children, Elizabeth, Michael, Steven, daughter-in-law Karen, and grandchildren Matthew, Caitlin and Ryan.

love,

Terri, John, Lauren and Jamie

Written Jan 29, 2011 6:28pm

So, after a long day at two ER's, John was just admitted to Brigham & Women's Hospital. He had a high fever yesterday and today, and had seizures this morning. The seizures were likely from the fever, and they are keeping him to figure out what is causing the fever. I will report again once I know more.

Written Feb 2, 2011 12:33pm

My last update was before I got to the hospital this morning. John's doctors now believe that he has an infection in his brain. He just went in for emergency surgery to find out what is going on for sure. It will be several hours before I know anything.

Written Feb 9, 2011 8:58am

I wanted to share some great news that we got last night...

The pathology report from the latest surgery showed "no evidence of viable tumor, only radiation necrosis". So, once his melon is healed a little, John will go back on the treatment plan that he was on (chemo 5 days, off 23).

He's feeling better each day, and is spending most of his time resting, which is what he needs right now.

Thanks for all of your support.

Written Feb 20, 2011 8:31am

We had a long visit with John's neuro-oncologist last week and discussed changing his treatment plan. The standard of care in Europe, where the largest studies of this cancer and treatment took place, is to follow up after 6 weeks of concurrent chemo and radiation with 6 monthly cycles of chemotherapy. For some reason, in the U.S. the standard has become 12 monthly cycles, but there is no evidence that patients having 12 cycles have better outcomes than those having 6. Since the pathology reports from John's last two surgeries were both positive (only radiation effect dead "necrotic" cells"), and because he's had so many issues related to treatment, we have decided to stop the chemotherapy after the 6th cycle.

So, John just finished his 6th maintenance cycle last night! His doctor will monitor him closely, with blood work, MRI's and appointments every few weeks. We are thrilled to have a break from treatment, and look forward to having John feel more like himself soon.

Written Jun 15, 2011 9:40am

We had a wonderful few days on Martha's Vineyard, leading up to Lauren and Ilan's wedding. The wedding was perfect. It was a beautiful day, and was so much fun.

Unfortunately, all of the excitement was too much for John and he had a seizure on the way home from the wedding. Somehow, during all of the commotion, he developed compression fractures in his back. This is common when someone is on steroids for a long time. It is extremely painful, which is why he is still in Martha's Vineyard Hospital. The treatment is rest and medication to manage the pain. So, we don't know how long he will be here yet.

Written Aug 21, 2011 9:59am

Well friends and family, here we go again. Halfway through our stay on Martha's Vineyard, John developed bleeding in his brain. He was med flighted from the Vineyard to Brigham & Women's, and had emergency surgery this morning to remove a blood clot that had developed from the bleeding.

He is out of surgery. The surgery was successful, they removed the whole clot and there is no further sign of bleeding. He's awake, alert and is doing well.

Written Sep 9, 2011 1:38pm

Update time...

John had an appointment today with his neurosurgeon. She reported that the pathology report from his last surgery showed no live tumor cells, so we are thrilled with that news.

Last week, he had a procedure to put an IVC filter in place. It was an outpatient procedure, and went well. The filter is there to block clots from going to his lungs or heart. Since he now has this, he won't have to be on blood thinners, so he's very happy not to have to give himself shots anymore.

Earlier this week, he landed in the hospital for a couple of days with abdominal pains. Everything serious was ruled out, and he's feeling better now. So, we are back to walking to build up his stamina to get ready for the Boston Brain Tumor walk on October 1st.

Written Oct 9, 2011 4:38pm

Hi,

John had his latest MRI this week, and the news was not great. It showed a lot more swelling in his brain than last time, and also some enhancement around the tumor site. They can't tell if it's radiation effect or if it's progression of the tumor, but it doesn't really matter right now, as we have to do something to treat the swelling.

So, this week, John will start a new treatment. He will receive Avastin infusions every other week. Avastin is not a chemotherapy drug. It works by blocking blood flow to the tumor site, and also is effective at reducing swelling. This should allow John the opportunity to come off of the steroids at some point too.

John's had his steroids bumped up until the Avastin treatment starts, which has helped with the headaches and head rushes that he was having. He's getting out and walking every day, especially in this beautiful weather, and is in good spirits.

So, that's the latest. I'll try to update later this week after his first infusion.

Written Oct 19, 2011 8:39pm

Sorry for the late update. We've spent the last week or so thinking about options. John had another MRI yesterday to try to give us more data. Unfortunately, the results were still confusing. One test seems to confirm tumor growth, while the other seems to indicate that the tumor is not active. John's doctor thinks it is most likely progression. The swelling is still quite significant too. So, today John had his first Avastin infusion. He will get them every other week. It doesn't take too long, and we've been told that people tolerate it very well. So, we have a plan, and have started treatment again, and we feel good about that.

Written Nov 17, 2011 6:37pm

John had an MRI yesterday, and we got some great news. Both the swelling and whatever was happening in the tumor area were dramatically reduced, after only two Avastin infusions. Dr. Norden was very pleased with the results, and we are too!

John is feeling really good. He's got more energy, and is able to be a little more active. He's having some cabin fever and enjoys getting out when he can. He would certainly enjoy going out for coffee or lunch, or even a walk, if any of you can work it into your schedules.

He had his third infusion yesterday, and we'll continue on this course. We are looking forward to spending the holidays with our family and wish you all a happy Thanksgiving.

Written Dec 26, 2011 8:37pm

I hope that you know how grateful we are for all of your support this year. I don't know how we could do this if it weren't for the help that we get from our family and friends.

John has continued with his treatment every other week, with a slight delay when he had a day surgery to have a port placed in his chest. This will make the infusions less painful. His spirits are good, and he has enjoyed getting out to see our wonderful family over the holidays, and to visit with friends too. We have loved having Lauren, Ilan, Jamie, and Jamie's boyfriend Isaac able to spend so much time with us.

I pray that 2012 will be a healthy year for all of us.

Written Apr 28, 2012 1:06pm

All, it's John:

I have been remiss with my updates and for that I apologize.

Health Update:

We all face challenges every day. I choose to focus on living and cannot overemphasize how important a strong positive attitude is. I am prepared to live a long time. I know there are a lot of people battling some tough diseases; please stay strong, you are in my thoughts and prayers. I also want to recognize the caregivers like Terri. They invest so much of themselves into the battle. It's so inspiring to witness so many people loving and living through so much. God bless you all.

My brother Charlie used to really like my stories. His only comment was that I calmed the stories down too much and should put more of the full story into my writing.

In honor of my wonderful big brother Charlie, who left us in December of 2010, I am writing this story in a full unabridged style with the salty language used in my boyhood home.

Everyone, particularly those going through hard times, needs something to bring a smile to their face. Hopefully you will find something worth smiling about.

This is a true story about my childhood. OK, it's about 90 to 95% true; I never let the facts get in the way of telling a good story.

Background:

It's the summer of 1957 and I just turned 4 years old. My father is a career navy man stationed in Rhode Island, currently at sea, but expected home any day for an extended stay, which always gave us nervous stomach aches.

Friday is shopping day. For some crazy reason, Friday is the only day of the week that the Nickerson contingent can go shopping, along with every other person in town. I always ask to be left home but my mother always tells me that I am too much work. I know that's crazy because my sister Kathy is two years older than me and has my brothers Bobby and Charlie scared stiff of her. She is like a Maine Coon cat so everyone gives her a pass.

I'm only 4, and I love to talk, which drives my grandfather insane. Here is a typical Friday afternoon grocery shopping trip.

It's Aunt Barbara, Aunt Margie, Aunt Carolyn, Grandma Nickerson aka Grandma Nick, my mom and the star, Grandpa Nick.

My aunts are all nice normal people that sit with me in the back of a 1953 Pontiac. My mom, Grandma Nick and Grandpa Nick all sit in front. Nobody ever says a word to Grandpa Nick because they are scared stiff of him: everyone but me that is. It was always a quiet ride to the grocery store because nobody could sense what was going to set Grandpa off, and off he would go.

Grandpa Nick's key characteristics and rules:

Grandpa loved the Boston Red Sox and listened to every game on the radio. When Ted Williams was in his prime, Grandpa loved that Williams got fined 250 dollars for spitting at the fans.

Grandpa's big life achievement was that he used one match a day to light his first unfiltered camel cigarette of the day, and never had to use another match all day as he chain smoked. He took great pride in that achievement and also loved cheap brandy, although not to excess.

Rules: Since Grandpa listened to the Red Sox on the radio, talking during the game was not allowed. Any question or comment that ran into the game was ignored. He ignored me. Grandpa Nick was old school. In retrospect, I think he was getting used to a post WW2 world with changing roles for women and men. At least I hope that explains some of his orneriness. Actually, I think he was born with a lemon in his mouth.

We arrived at the grocery store and before Grandpa Nick could speak, Grandma says, "Johnny is staying in the car with you", and "it will be good to spend some time with your grandson".

Have you ever felt a pair of eyes drilling a white hot hole in the back of your head? I don't mean a little ticked off, I mean a full on head drilling? Well that was Grandpa, in fact Grandpa always called me by three words: sons of bitches (sob).

The first words out of Grandpa were, "I want you to sit in back with your mouth shut and listen to the game." My response was, "I want to come sit with you in front." Grandpa says yes, but only if I don't talk. I agree and promptly hop in front. I really tried to be quiet but it's hard for a little guy to be quiet, especially during a ball game. To his credit, Grandpa warned me several times with "sons of bitches" and was about to kick me into the back seat when he started with a terrible cough. It was the kind of cough only a lifelong smoker of unfiltered cigarettes can get. It must have lasted two or three minutes. It was so deep it scared me terribly. After Grandpa regained his composure and the game went to commercial, I summoned up my courage and asked Grandpa if he was going to die? He responded with, "of course, everyone dies" and I said, "I meant, are you going to die today"? He was angry and kicked me into the back seat. I did not understand that response to a good question, so I told Grandpa that he was mean, and it was due to his itchy burning hemorrhoids, as seen on TV. That was the first time I ever saw my Grandpa smile.

The ride home from shopping was quiet, except for me. The Red Sox were at commercial, so the timing was perfect. I cleared my throat and said, "Mom, where did I come from"? The car fell deathly silent. I expected my mom to say, "Chelsea Naval Hospital", but mom and all the passengers thought I was asking the big question.

Without hesitation Grandpa said, "one day I was driving down the road and saw the devil flying. The devil crapped you out and I swung the car over to catch you. I drove you home for your mom. Luckily it wasn't trash day or there would be no Johnny".

The car erupted in laughter. It was a great sound, plus it was the first time I saw my Grandma and Grandpa hold hands and smile.

To be continued…

Written May 4, 2012 8:48pm

Hi it's John again!

It is late Friday afternoon, about a week after the last episode with grandpa. My mother has just looked out the window and seen me covered in dirt from head to toe. Her first words were, "how did you get so dirty?" Followed with, "you're taking a bath tonight. Supper is soon, don't go ANYWHERE" and "you're too dirty to come in the house". That left me with one idea. I would go next door to Grandma Nick's house. She always welcomed a visit, plus she always had chocolate and coca cola. Since she lived next door, all I had to do was walk down to the end of the house, take a left, and walk down the lawn and bingo, I'm at grandma's. I had to go quick so mom wouldn't catch me. So I ran quickly and got to the front of grandma's house. I was so happy because I hadn't seen grandma all day and she would have treats.

As I approached the house I could see someone leaning against a screen and it didn't look like grandma. As I got closer I could smell a stinky old cigarette and I heard someone yelling and swearing at the radio. It could only be one person and that was Grandpa Nick. I was crushed. Goodbye grandma hugs. Goodbye grandma candy. Goodbye coca cola.

 I had to think quickly. Maybe grandma was in another room. I continued to walk by my grandpa and said "hi grandpa". Without hesitation he said, "There's nobody home. Go away". I said, "Grandpa, you're home". He said, no, I'm not". I said, "Yes, you are. I'll come visit you". I was thinking about candy or maybe coke.

I must have caught grandpa in a rare good mood because he said yes. I was stunned and surprised because he never let me in. I walked to the end of the driveway and took a right up the walkway to the screened door. The door was unlocked. I was glad. Little did I know that I'd need to make an emergency escape later.

I walked in and before I could say hi, Grandpa said "no talking during the Sox." I waited until a commercial and got right down to business. "Grandpa, do you have any coke or chocolate"? He immediately said, "Is that why you came here, to talk me out of treats?" I felt a little guilty. I said "no Grandpa". He said, "Good, you can have a butterscotch". My least favorite candy, but candy none the less. I took it from the dish and popped it into my mouth. The Red Sox were back and I had to shut up.

Just then I heard my mother call my name, "Johnny", in her special sing song voice that was half loving and half get home pronto. It meant supper was served. My poor mother was such a lady. Serving dinner to our family was like feeding a pack of feral dogs; no saying grace; no talking; just gorging. I said, "Bye Grandpa" and started to go. He said, "What's for supper?" I said, "It's Friday, so it's fish sticks and tater tots". He looked at me disgustedly and said, "You Catholics".

He returned to the Sox as I started to leave. I stopped and said, "After supper I'll come back and sit with you". He said, "Don't bother. I've had enough of you today". That really hurt my feelings. Without thinking I said, "I've had enough of you too". That was a really ballsy stupid move. My mother had told me 100 times, "Don't sass Grandpa or you'll be sorry". Out of the corner of my eye I saw the old man move as quick as a cat. He grabbed his cane. Luckily, I was already heading towards the screen door. I ran as fast as I could. Thank god the emergency screen door was unlocked. I burst out the door just in time to hear the cane crash into the door. He missed my head by an inch. Now I knew why I shouldn't sass my grandpa. As I ran home I heard two things; Grandpa picking up the telephone and Grandpa swearing, "sons of bitches".

It was a short run home. My mother had a rule; no running with candy in your mouth. Lots of kids choked to death every year because of running with candy in their mouths. I stopped, took the butterscotch out of my mouth and put it into in my pocket for later. Then I realized I had a handful of dirt in each pocket. I always had to check my pockets for toads and salamanders after a particularly sad mistake at the dinner table.

I had to walk up the stairs and through the screen door. My mom was already on the phone with Grandpa. The conversation was, "Yes, I'll fix you a plate" and "come right over. Don't worry. I'll speak with Johnny". I knew then I was screwed. My mother looked at me sternly and she realized how dirty I was. She said, "I have to talk to you about Grandpa but first, how did you get so dirty?" I said, "no toads or salamanders in my pockets". Mom said again, "How did you get so dirty?" I picked up on her frustration. I sensed I would get spanked. I'd been in the back yard and I'd found a big toad and a good place to dig. Once I told her most of the truth she lost interest and told me to wash up for supper.

I went into the bathroom to wash up. I had a unique understanding of washing up. I would use my right hand to get the water dripping then put my left hand under the water for two seconds. No soap, no right hand done. My rationale was I only used my left hand because I'm a lefty. I ran out of the bathroom for fish sticks and tater tots. By then the feral dog feeding frenzy was over. It was just my dad, mom, and me. Dad was taking my tater tots which I hated anyway. Mom finally saw my right hand and said, "go wash both hands and use hot water and soap".

There were lots of ways to earn a spanking in my house. The most serious offense was lying or being sassy, followed by minor things like swearing or not coming when called, or taking candy without asking etc.

Mom had gone to grandpa's and she came back very angry. All she said was, "Bob start running the tub for Johnny. We are going to talk in the bedroom". I followed mom into the bedroom. I asked, "Are we gonna heat some water"? We had the crappiest water heater in town. It heated enough water for a very small cup of luke warm tea. After that it was like a cold mountain stream. Mom was punishing me for being sassy. Once in the bedroom I felt like a trapped mouse. She looked at me and I knew I was in big trouble. Before I could speak mom said to forget about dessert and she found the butterscotch candy stuck in my shorts. "Why did you sass Grandpa"? I broke down in tears and said, "Grandpa hurt my feelings". I tried to tell her the whole story, but she quickly lost interest. She told me to toughen up, take your cold bath, wash everything with soap and water, clean the tub and then go right to bed. That was a cold bath. I tried to do everything right. I even did a good job of brushing my teeth.

I jumped into bed and announced I was ready for mom to hear my prayers. My sister popped into the room and announced that I was being punished, that mom liked my brothers more than me and that Grandpa was probably gonna kill me tomorrow for being so sassy. Just then mom came in and said to my sister, "What are you doing here?" My sister said, "Oh, Johnny just asked me to come in". Mom said, "please go; he's got to say his prayers". I knelt on the floor and said a Hail Mary and Our Father, an act of contrition. Mom said it was time for bed. I was desperate to stall. The only tactic I could think of was a funny prayer so I announced to mom I had a really funny prayer and did she want to hear it? She said no then paused and asked if there were any dirty words or any bad things? I said "no". She said, "say it quickly". "Now I lay me down to sleep I pray the lord my soul to keep. If I should die before I wake I pray the lord my toys to break." Mom smiled and said, "good night. You're still being punished. Go to sleep". I said, "But you didn't spank me." She said, "It's not too late".

I fooled around in bed for five minutes and then I had to go to the bathroom so I got out of bed and headed towards the bathroom. Mom said, "Get back to bed. If you take one more step I'll break your ass". Without hesitation I said, "Dad told me everyone has a cracked ass". Mom said, "Don't say that. Get back to bed." I did, but I was in trouble because I had spent a lot of the day drinking from a stream that my neighbor had warned me about and now my tummy hurt badly. I was in trouble.

Written Jun 18, 2012 3:42pm

Last week, John started a new treatment. It's called Novocure TTF. It involves placing transducer arrays on the skin near the brain tumor site. The device uses electric fields to disrupt the division of the cancer cells. I don't really understand why, but it doesn't affect the regular cells. It's FDA approved, and in clinical trials had results that were about the same as other forms of chemotherapy, but without the toxicity. He has to wear the device around the clock, and keep it on at least 18 hours a day. Ideally, it would be on for closer to 21-22 hours per day.

So, he has to carry the device and a battery pack when he leaves the house. We have lots of spare batteries. He also can plug into a wall charger when he's home and resting in his chair or bed. We have to shave his head every few days, and change the arrays at that time. There's quite a learning curve, but we are both adjusting. Here's a link to the website, if you want to learn more about it.

http://www.novottftherapy.com/

He will continue with the Avastin treatment every other week.

We are hopeful that both of these treatments will allow him to continue to feel good.

Written Aug 8, 2012 7:13pm

Hi,

John had his MRI yesterday, and both of his neuro-oncologists feel that his tumor is STABLE! I'm not surprised, as he's been feeling really well lately, but I'm glad to have the MRI as proof.

We don't know if this good news is due to the increased dose of Avastin he's now getting, or the Novocure TTF device, or some combination of both. Whatever it is, we're happy!

We've had a lot of issues with the Novocure during this hot summer. Evidently it's been overheating, which causes it's alarm to go off. John now calls it "Novo-suck". It's been a pretty time consuming effort, but I'm getting faster at shaving his head and changing out the arrays. It's super sensitive to sunlight, as those of you who've been around us at all know. It also responds negatively to sweat, and who could help sweating in the heat and humidity we've had. The doctor today told us we only had about 4 more weeks of hot weather. I asked him if he was a meteorologist as well as a neuro-oncologist?

Written Nov 17, 2012 7:57am

Hi everyone,

John and I are thrilled to welcome our first grandchild, a girl, named Mia Cynthia Behm. She arrived yesterday morning, weighed 7 lbs 13 oz, and is perfect! Mom, Dad and Mia are all doing well. Grandparents are over the moon!

love,

Written Dec 5, 2012 6:58pm

Hi family & friends,

This is a hard post to write, and I probably wouldn't be doing it yet, except that John has asked me to.

He had an MRI last Friday. Unfortunately, it showed tumor growth. He's also had some new symptoms, but mostly feels good. Today, we had a long talk with John's doc about his options.
There are several, but none of them will likely extend his life, and all will have tough side effects. We are taking some time to think about options, including stopping treatment, or just continuing with the current treatment.

We don't really know what this all means, but we'll keep you posted. Thanks for all of your support.

Written Jan 30, 2013 2:51pm

Hi,

More bad news. Today's MRI was not good. Not really a surprise, but there was significant tumor growth, and the tumor is now starting to grow into the left side of the brain. Since it is progressing pretty quickly, we decided not to continue with the Avastin treatments, and to call in hospice. We will not need to go back to Dana Farber. It was very difficult to say goodbye to Dr. Norden and his nurses. It felt so final. We are grateful that Jamie was able to be with us at this appointment. She was a great support, especially for me.

We don't know what this means in terms of time, but we are all certainly noticing changes in John's ability to use his left side, and expect that will continue to get worse. Dr. N. said we will probably notice more cognitive changes too.

We haven't spoken with hospice yet, so we don't know yet what suggestions they will make for accommodations at our house. I am very concerned about the stairs, and about John's inability to recognize his deficiencies. The last thing we need is a fall. Anyway, we will sort it out.

We are here and welcome visits with advance notice.

Written Feb 16, 2013 7:16am

So far, our experience with hospice has been very positive. When we lost our power in the storm last weekend, we went to our sister-in-law Elaine's house for the duration. Our hospice arranged for John to be seen by a local hospice nurse while we were there, and they also sent in an aide and a hospital bed.

We are back at home and are getting into a routine, with the nurse coming twice a week, an aide coming several days a week, the physical therapist, social worker and chaplain coming occasionally. They even brought over a rose for John on Valentine's day.

Our friends first turned our dining room/office into a bedroom for both of us, and then, when we were at Elaine's, moved everything again to set us up in the living room, so that John could have the TV. There were many years of dust behind the furniture and everything sparkles now!

John is spending most of his time in bed, but the physical therapist taught us how to transfer him from bed to wheelchair so that he can have a change of scenery. It's still scary for me, as he's pretty wobbly, but we will do it as long as we can. He can't walk any more due to his left side neglect. He is still ridiculously strong though, and is in good spirits. He loves doing the crossword puzzle daily, but can't write since he's a lefty. Our good friend Cindy has been doing them with him, and Elaine and I have tried too. It's not really my thing, but he's still very good at it.

I just wanted to let you know how things were going. I don't have words to describe how brave John has been, and continues to be.

Written Mar 31, 2013 9:45pm

Hello,

We are so very sad to have to tell you all that John passed this afternoon. He seemed comfortable and peaceful. Jamie, Lauren, Ilan and I were at his bedside, sharing tears and laughter, as he would have wanted. We are relieved that after three years, he can finally rest.

love,

Terri

30090842R00038